# Faultlines

## Caroline Maldonado

*to David, poet,
editor + fellow
Italianist!
best wishes
Caroline*

Published by Dempsey & Windle under their VOLE imprint


15 Rosetrees
Guildford
Surrey
GU1 2HS
UK
01483 571164
dempseyandwindle.com

A catalogue record for this book is available from the British Library

British Library Cataloguing-in-Publication Data:

ISBN: 978-1-913329-67-9

Printed and bound in the UK

## Acknowledgements

Acknowledgements and thanks are due to the editors of the following publications in which versions of these poems have appeared: *Shearsman; Orbis; Envoi; Iota; Artemis; Poetry Salzburg Review; The New European; The Morning Star; The New Walk; Tears in the Fence; Acumen; Agenda; Coast to Coast to Coast;* and the following anthologies: Smokestack Books' *Poems for John Berger* ( 2017); Second Light Publication's *Fanfare* (2015); Templar Poetry's *Octopus* (2012); and online in *London Grip, The High Window* and *Mediterranean Poetry.* Six poems have appeared in a pamphlet published by Indigo Dreams Publishing, 2014, *What they say in Avenale.*

'Mario' was a prize-winner in *Poetry on the Lake*'s *International Poetry Competition 2012.* A version of 'Kite-surfer' won first prize in *SPM Publication's Poetry Competition 2013.*

With special thanks to Mimi Khalvati for her guidance and to the friends who have made suggestions on these poems and given encouragement along the way, especially Mandy Pannett, Owen Gallagher, Ruth Valentine and Aviva Dautch.

And thanks to my publisher, Janice Dempsey, particularly for her professionalism, patience and good humour throughout.

# The Poems

## I  Faultlines

## II The Creek Men

## III Interiors

# I    Faultlines

## Mario

He ploughs early through the hot summer.
In the dark his lamp is lighting clods inch by inch.
Over the tractor he hears the first cockerel.

Daybreak picks out edges: a roofline, tower, spire,
while the moon's crescent slicks chalk on blue,
its arc finger-smudged. The one-eyed cat sleeps.

Now the sun is climbing the house wall and over
the hills, fine as silver paper, gleams the sea.
Mario switches off his lamp. Half a field to go.

**Horses above the lake of Cingoli.**

The sheen on their golden necks!
They come flying to greet me,
   twenty or more.

Black forests above, and below
the valley where clouds lap green water
   like wolves.

Later they nod their heads
against the flies that bathe
   in the rims of their deep eyes.

Two or three stand side by side,
lean their haunches into one another;
   one bends her back leg,

she points a hoof and
shifts her weight.
   One always stands alone.

Their noses are soft as doves,
their lips pass like shadows
   across my palm.

Light burns into the trees, the sky
darkens and, balanced on their points,
   the stars are riding bareback.

## On the eve of Ferragosto

the accordionist was playing and Guido
whose wife had recently died
was led by his sister

and they two-stepped
slowly around the stage
set up outside the church

under a full white moon
and his son stood watching
watched them dancing

till someone gave him a tube of bubbles
and he drew in his breath
and blew his heart into the wire O

which he held up high
for the wind to blow through
and dancers were turning

in the globules of light
the night wind rose and bubbles
streamed through the wire circle

unstoppable and dancers
stage, church and village all lifted
to meet the white moon.

## Pilgrims

The Devil's Gorge, they called it:
Cross here and you risk your life –

we bent and drank and crossed that bridge,
rusty tears on our foreheads and wet rock

against our palms, *la rocca lacrimosa*.
We'd left silhouettes along the skyline

of our cars and caravans, the tourist stalls
and a roadside crucifix, fading in the dusk,

some of us weak as chickens, others
young and strong, we carried on, up now

on the other side, lifting the ones who fell.
They'd warned us she lived there, cast out

from Cumae until the end of time, and how
she lured young knights to her sibylline cave

into the scented arms of her attendants
- the gentlest of maids who, Fridays at midnight,

transmuted into serpents, livid and blind.
Of course none of us believed such a tale

but we followed the trail in single file,
each after our own private prophecy.

The summit was pitted with scrub and thorn.
Shadows of eagle and buzzard swept over us

in pursuit of their small warm prey
and hours later a mute goatherd signed us the way

to a hermit's hut where we spent a night
more silent than any we had known.

For days we wandered, afraid, our path lost
but we returned, every one of us, and we were changed

though could not speak of it, neither what we sought
nor if we'd found it, where we'd been or why.

## Sirocco

They tried to shut it out, the hot African wind.
All night it raged.  It snapped tree-trunks,
clattered shutters and lifted deckchairs
and umbrellas across the lawn.

Now it has burst through the door:
dry leaves, dust and detritus bounce
and skitter across the floor tiles,
tossed like small boats across the sea.

## The musician in Naples

On a low wall in a church square
on the edge of the city
the Tuareg musician says:

'Two hundred in a fifty foot boat.
Crushed in the motor room, we couldn't
breathe. Twenty five died.

The last of the bottled water we gave
 to the children and when help came
we handed up the babies first.

In a hostel near the station
they give us coupons for food.
Each morning we stand guard

by a sheet on the pavement
and peddle our wares,
a jacket, old trainers, a phone.

I used to walk for hours in the desert.
I was blessed with solitude.
The land and I were one'.

## Libycum Mare

i)

A water goddess from the sea off Alexandria
has risen after a thousand years – the lips
on her pink granite head curved with a hint
of a smile as if she predicted her benign future –
and hoisted to her full five-metre height
in this museum she exhibits all the majesty
of the deity she once was in her ancient city
before it sank in its archipelago of silt.
But when the diver found her, touched a thigh
an arm, a cheek, while fish streamed in a shoal
round marble columns that still reached for skies,
when he scraped the sediment off, helped roll
her round to face our world with open eyes,
did she shrink back, witness to the future toll?

ii)

The sea between Alexandria and Crete
tips up dinghies, spills out their cargo,
summons a hundred and seventeen lives below
to stock its own museum. Record this date.
A mother holds her baby high to be saved
before she drowns; a man sinks like a column,
like a statue, but not for him a resurrection;
no human limb is fashioned with granite's weight
nor is soft flesh preserved in metres of silt.
Their corpses like buoyant wood are swept by waves.
Today all along the shoreline they drift.
A fisherman comes upon their sandy grave,
returns to shroud each body with a cloth
as more emerge, not one of them with breath.

## Emanuel

His name was Emanuel: *God is with us*.
When Boko Haram trashed their home

and hacked their child to pieces
he and Chinyery packed up their pain

with their possessions and put one
hope before the other to Libya

across the sea to Lampedusa, to Fermo
where a Catholic mission took them in.

*Monkey* was the mugger's cry, a metal post
his weapon. Chinyeri gathers her friends

around her and sings. Her voice comes from
who knows where and goes to some other place.

She will wash her man's body ready for burial.
She will drink the water she washed him in.

## Patriotism

Watch out for this man
mounting the steps
of the Monument
to the Fallen,
the tricolour flag
round his shoulders,
his right arm raised
in a Roman salute.

He's left bullets
in the stone wall,
six bodies crumpled
on the pavement
not far from the market
where Africans
hawk their wares
in Piazza della Libertà.

## Prospecting

'Beyond the ploughed field,
see the oak?' The boy gestures
down the valley towards the place

you could so easily miss
where his friend discovered
a stack of coins, gold — each one

worth thousands. Then he fishes out
his own finds, a *madonnina* plaque
dating back five hundred years

and some coins. 'So far down
I had to dig', he said, 'and in this heat!'
Yet how close to us they lie.

I hold a coin, cool in my palm,
bronze, with the worn profile
of some imperial Caesar.

## All out to sea

Flies fret and squabble on the window pane,
feral cats stroll past my door after
tit-bits or company or a sip from the water
I always leave them in a pan under the vine.
Across the sky the drama of buzzard and crow
plays out again. Today it's the crows that win
and the buzzard departs.  Who knows, next time?
 – the crow guarding her nest has most to lose.
The carrion crow takes a turn with an eye
on my neighbour's chicks; doves head off to confess
in the woods; a harlequin bee-eater sashays
on gusts of wind and redstarts, blue-tits and finches
forage and feast and hurry about their business
as if this were their world ruled from on high!

My lawn needs mowing, but leaving it for now
I step through clover, daisies and celandine
abundant under the olive.  I'll let grow
the wild mint and fennel and when it's time
tear the leaves for seasoning into a pan
for my evening meal. Until then, my eyes
will dine on poppies and the hoopoe's fan,
its open crest spread wide shooing flies
and on the swallow, bee-eater and turtle dove
who have hills as backdrop, sky their runway.
But how last night that sky roared and cracked,
spat hail and smashed gravel from the road above!
Or were those lacerations far away,
the storm elsewhere, another country hacked?

Branches lie heaped in bundles on the ground.
Their leaves will be sun-dried to feed the lambs
but now, to me, they resemble funerary mounds.
'This big it was,' he says and parts his hands,
'when I was ten – a metre wide or more.
Each year we'd put a basket in its fork,
with nylon for cover, filled with hay to store
apples through the year.' The mulberry's trunk
is ridged and desiccated like long-baked earth;
the stumps, sawed to the collar, dusty, hollow;
they bleed sap. The branches were snapped by storms
and, without hard-pruning, others would have gone.
Now the wounds will heal and the scar tissue
form and a dormant bud prepare for birth.

Again, sleepless at dawn, sat by my pot
of basil I look out to sea, but no longer
recognise the view.  All the familiar
landmarks are gone, the world altered overnight,
the solid relationship between land
and sky askew.  I went to bed in foothills
of a mountain chain and woke up on an island;
the mists are waves and all the other hills
an archipelago. Slowly, slowly the mists
dry off: the scene below is known to me now,
the oak clumps, Loreto's dome, homesteads,
and in the new light I observe how
cruelly the sea's fine substance can harden
from liquid to a bar of hammered platinum.

## Wolf

Late evening I saw you, wolf,
trotting before me,

all alone on the road
nobody uses any more.

Then you were gone
high up beyond the juniper

and flowering judas.
People told me

there were no more wolves
in the forests.

In breaking daylight
the farmer called on his son to help him.

Together they piled one
torn sheep on the other.

## Kite-surfer

O how you skim the water, lean on air and turn into wind,
your kite above you like a segment of moon!

Riding the waves encased in your harness, your feet
strapped to your board, you twist up against the sky.

We watch from the sands, our hearts reaching high, willing
you further as you lift from water and vanish into light.

But now - do you fall? Each one of us thinks of what's
failing
or failed, dying or on the brink: we mourn our lost rapture.

A long while you lie prostrate on water until the moon
loops and climbs and lifts you in its shadow.

**Fault**

Under the Eternal City, bones
have long since crumbled
past all sorrow in caverns
of *porzellana* & *tufo*
that after millenia still hold up
& barely feel the shudders

of Visso where Earth reaches out
to the welcoming air, rips open
the mountain's crust as if to flay
its own burning skin, a self-
flagellating Marsyas, careless of
flying rock & timbers,

stone & plaster, careless
of those small breathing
creatures not yet ready to go.

## The breach

At 3.36 the earth heaves us on its back and strikes
our bed-head against the stone wall like a gong.
We leave our doors open when we run. Arquata
del Tronto, Amatrice, Accumoli are dragged down.

A *campanile* slants over rubble, its clock-hands stuck
at 3.38 by which time a child's gone, one foot shoeless;
a son on leave from his good job in Rome, aunts,
cousins, gone. Hilltop towns a war-zone.

Elisabetta leaps from a second floor balcony,
her father catches her in his arms and can't let go.
A grey-robed, blood-streaked nun calls *Un angelo!*
when a dusty wingless lad pulls her free.

Tectonic plates approach Europe; Le Marche
moves northeast to Venice. Lazio shifts
in the same direction but lags behind.
Our past and future fall in. Now, in a hostel,

refugees donate their 'pocket money'.
Volunteers scrape at granite and travertine,
like tracker dogs they must learn to sense a pulse.

## Out of time

The floor lifted and our bed
slithered and bucked against its stall
as Our Own Correspondent,
without a break, reported on Kashmir.

Giancarlo and his family took refuge
in the furthest corners of their courtyard.
Others gathered in the main street
or shivered in cars through the night.

Amatrice tumbled into a crevice.
You soon fell back asleep.
I sat in the kitchen drinking tea
awaiting the after-shock.

### We live on a restless planet

a sense of slip

throws up    heaves out

strike-slip dip-slip


time & space  split

mountains dense  with fault lines

our apennines


where has it  gone

our horizon

## Visso

'Visso. Never forget my name.
Voices breathe through my crevices
scrambled with fennel and mallow.
My stonecutters chiselled the serpents
that curve, skin to skin, over this broken doorway.
Woodcarvers polished to a sheen
the Redeemer Christ bringing both humble
and arrogant to their knees in hard times.
I cultivated thinkers, schooled them in logic
and philosophy, apprenticed artists
to embody their dreams in chapels and palaces.
My castellated walls shielded soldiers
and shopkeepers. I gave birth to a Pope.'

A town without people.
Now the schools have fallen,
where will the children learn?

Church roofs have imploded,
their frescoes exposed to rain,
where will the people pray?

The walls of their homes fallen in,
kitchens smashed to rubble,
where can they house their memories?

One year on and nothing's been done.
Domenico the shepherd's still in his caravan,
every few months moving his flock
between high pastures and low valleys.
Pierino and Rosa, now in their eighties,

live in a shed. They're prepared to wait,
are used to a simple life, but last winter's
snow and frost and this summer's
African heat have been hard to take.

One year on but this has changed:
On the outskirts, close to a clear lake fed
by the icy, fast-flowing Nera, tents are set up,
cubicles for temporary toilets, pine huts,
a bar selling cappuccinos, fresh pastry.
At lunch for six euro they offer lasagne,
pizza in the evenings. No festival but
there will be music and dancing tonight.
In here you can buy cuts of wild boar hams,
salamis and sheep's cheese. You'll find maps,
postcards recalling Piazza Martiri Vissani,
the great collegiate church, Palazzo dei Priori.

Monte Vettore, Devil's Peak,
Monte Sibilla, Hell's Throat:
see them rise over the clouds,
violet, insubstantial, innocent,

while on a rock above the forest
a chamois goat (the year before last
nearly extinct) holds her balance
then descends, guiding her young.

**When time is lost**

Once this town was hung
with ensigns and gonfalons.
Courtiers paraded their horses
caparisoned round the piazza
and back street bargains
were struck for a purse of florins.

Last week card-playing elders
strung out their time under the loggia.
A woman in the market eased down
her basket with potatoes, carrots
and celery for the minestrone,
to hail a friend just passing by.

You can look into her living room now,
its sofa white with dust,
the midday sun clambering
through broken glass to cast
patterns on the floor and flash
indecipherable codes on the mirror

and into her kitchen, long table bare,
copper pots in rows along a wall,
a calendar no longer legible,
sideboard with spoons
sunk in a bowl of rubble
and on the stove a coffee pot.

Today brick and stone
are smashed back into earth.
Houses are propped against
sheered hills like abandoned
theatre sets with half-rooms,
quarter-rooms, hanging.

## Trees hold fast

We drive into the mountains
past two-storey houses
propped with scaffolding
and bars with vacant car parks,
past the restaurant we lunched in
last year, now closed,
to where the ascent begins,
the road ends, pastureland
rolls away and below us
the skyline wavers in the sun.

In these pine forests
the roots of trees held fast,
breathing with the earth
as it rose and fell,
but the ski lift is broken
and the five hotels,
curtains still at their windows,
are boarded up with signs
to keep out, warning us,
just passing, not to pry.

**And next, as a consequence of the tremors,
came the avalanche**

Fifty-eight hours in the underworld
- a punishment? A foretaste of what was
to be our absurd and final fate, hurled

into hell with half-full water bottles
on a snooker table and five jars of Nutella?
Adults and children, we counted sixteen of us.

Some cried, some comforted the weak. Stranger
quickly became friend: when our cheeks were sore
from the glacial air we touched - a reminder

of the feel of another's skin or simply for
reassurance that we were still alive.
Then all the phone batteries died: no more

messages to wait for. And the flashlights
gone, too. Surely that was the worst of it,
the dark. Or was it our thirst (we sucked on ice)

or the silence?  What had we done to deserve it?
Where was the justice? Pointless questions mumbled
to each other, the answers coming too late.

There were those among us who crumbled
all at once (just like the innocent mountain
suddenly stripped of all its power now tumbled

so close over our heads) and in their confusion,
believing we had no future, they knelt down,
spilled imaginary crimes, prayed for salvation.

Then there were the rest of us who found
no such relief but we raised our voices
to whoever might listen.  Guided by sound,

we struck out at the walls with snooker cues,
rattled wedged-shut doors and windows and clanged
the chairs - anything to be heard. We chose

songs that all could share -  the ones partisans
sang came soonest to our minds as if we
too were bound by a worthy cause.  A bang,

muffled, heard only by a child, that she
at first dismissed yet kept straining to hear,
became a hope although still we could see

nothing and no hope could counter the fear.
We waited, immobile, breath held tight in our chests,
until a dog's bark found us through the air.

There was talk of miracles, of how we were blessed,
when they hauled us out, so weak and defenceless.

## The intercession

For the bridge's re-opening
   the first to cross were the Mayor
in his red, white and green sash,
   local dignitaries, press photographers,
then the priest who sent off the *madonnina*

with a prayer – and off she went
   swinging from the joist down along
the bridge's third supporting column.
   She caught her balance, hand raised
to bless us who watched from the lakeside

   and the leaping carp and the stream
of catfish dreaming through the shallows.
   Hoisted far from the midday sun
into the still water, she blessed the cool
   green element she moved through

as three divers guided her down
   and bound her fast in the cold dark silt
where she will live unseen, protecting
   all who pass, protecting the bridge
from whatever down there cracked it.

## Cracks

For months I have written poems
about cracks in the earth.  I have
felt the stone walls of my home
tremble and visited hill-top towns,
the heart of them smashed to rubble.
I have tried and failed to find
a meaning in such sudden endings.

After weeks of drought the grass
is sodden, grey clouds slouch
over the horizon, shot through
with one shaft of light as if a crack
in the heavens were opening
but the sky can offer nothing now
to Max, in a coma with his skull split.

## Water, now

When the sky's harsh blue fades and day's dry heat
declines and we step outside and view the damage
to field and flowerbed from lack of water
after months without rain, when a fountain
is every night's waking dream, we watch life
wither and pour out our last glass of wine.

This year's harvest will bring us no more wine.
Our grapes are shrivelled by the summer heat.
Not even the wild boar comes to feed and its life
too hangs in the balance.  Proof of our damage
lies everywhere and yet we dream of fountains
and our riverbeds still gushing with water.

We thought it would gush forever, water.
For can't our Mediterranean, dark as wine
and free, renew itself and our fountains
despite bloated seasons and searing heat?
How ignorant we were of the damage
we caused, how careless we've been with our life.

Though we're young, we look back on our life
like old people, recall what we've lost. Water
haunts us. With weapons primed we do damage
to one another. Rather than drink wine
with friends we drain their reservoirs, before heat
numbs us, then we sleep and dream of fountains.

How they sweetened our Roman squares, those fountains:
Bernini's boat swept from the Tiber, a life
of marble horses, turtles, rinsed clean.  In the heat
we lifted our skirts and paddled in Trevi's water,
heads tilted, mouths open to catch more wine
spilled by spouting gods, oblivious to the damage.

In a mad bacchanal, we hoped that somehow the damage
would dissolve, would wash away in the fountains
of our dreams.  We drank to forget (when barrels of wine
were filled to the brim) and gorged on myths that life
could carry us like the boat on Tiber's water
and we would never again suffer such heat.

Our wine's finished and evening has drunk the heat.
We must confront the damage: where's our water?
Where, our fountains? What's become of our life?

## Regina Aquarium

Turn off the taps
in this city built on water.
We're all dried up.

Thieves have left
their siphons, their tubing
and pressure pumps

by drained reservoirs.
In the days of water
sun split particles

of light through spray
in the fountains
where marble gods

guided a torrent
with only one hand
and Keats might have heard

the splash of Bernini's boat
before it bore him away
on a last pulse of water.

## Moka

To make a good *moka*, aim to get the balance
between coffee and water right. Fill the base
of the metal pot with liquid only so far, leaving
space for the valve under the rim to breathe.

Tamp the ground beans with the back of a spoon,
screw on the top and place the pot on the flame.
A gentle bubbling soon starts but it still has a while
to go, time for you to dry and stack the plates.

The steam's building up. When the coffee's nearly
ready, through a narrow funnel the vapour shoots out.
It screams with the sound lava might make

when it strains to break free of the earth and spouts
ash over churches and kitchens alike, rendering
redundant all images of piety and the drying of plates.

## Museo Piersanti

In her workshop the restorer steadies
her paintbrush under the spotlight,
its fine hairs barely touching the panel,

the blue robe of the mother.
In a dark corner behind her, life-sized,
eyes closed, lies a carving of the son.

His pale skin with only reflected light
takes on a polished sheen revealing
pinpricks of woodworm, blood-drops

on his chest and the matt white streaks
where rubble from a stricken church
has scraped away its surface.

In the next room hangs one figure
among others salvaged from ruins,
polychromal, stern and open-eyed

on his cross, *Il Cristo Trionfante.*
Since the first brush of paint on wood
he's had a thousand years to witness

life and death, the struggles of rebel earth,
crumbling churches and museums
such as this palazzo – its *piano nobile*

closed but the collection mostly saved
by three young women who donned
hard hats to enter *la zona rossa.*

They combed through rubble while
after-shocks made the region tremble,
picked out broken torsos, torn canvases.

Then came the architects and conservators
and the volunteers who still arrive
daily to sweep the courtyard under

the great fig tree that was pruned back
so hard nobody expected it to live.
Now the museum doors are open.

Strung up over the courtyard, wall to wall,
are umbrellas, pink and lemon, sky-blue,
and where their shadows fall, mosaics bloom.

# II    The Creek Men

## The Creek Men

i)

Through a cracked torso
light splits, wind
streams from the east.

I watch you lift
mud and straw
from reed-beds,
stitch back
a lost arm with
hemlock fronds.

Toads hide under
your giant's feet,
insects spatter
on its damp neck.

See the gap
in the crux of
knee and elbow,
how the armature
reaches out through
clay hand to sky.

ii)

First you modelled him from clay
and after you'd finished and he lay
in your studio cast hard and whole,
you stroked his chest and forehead,
continued to tend him like a doctor
his patient, while the wind sifted
dust though the cracked window
and called him through the reeds.

Were they hot wax tears he wept
when you left him in marshland?
Flat on his back, a perch for gulls
and herons, he now contemplates
our ancestors - not those kitted out
like kings sepulchred with bounty
in a ship's hold — but the others
chucked loose in a common grave.

iii)

If I lived in that storehouse overlooking the creek
I'd walk out all hours through the reed-beds
under the busy skies, avoiding the deepest troughs
where you can sink up to your knees
towards the rowing boat at the water's edge,
there to see the man prone on mudflats,
head slightly lifted to view the horizon.

Later the sea, directed by the moon,
will reach over the bronze figure, lap by lap.
He'll lie underwater as if he'd never been.
And when the sea slacks again and streams away
I'll be back to see him resurrected on his mound
sun-whitened under the guano of gulls.

iv)

The hawk on a weathervane
by the replica bridge turns
its head from side to side.

It looks real. I stand quite still.

A pregnant sheep, her legs
pointing crookedly up,
struggles to get right but can't.

A pike, two foot long,
lies with open jaw, killer fangs
and black holes, eyes sucked dry.

The creek men aren't dead.
They're rooted and ready.

One presses against the wind.
Another leans on his branch
to hold up. He looks like mud.

v)

They are the creek men. Carcass-carriers,
grown out of reeds, forged from mud,
twigs, leaf-litter.

Their lives are mudflats, their history marshland,
tides and sky. From daybreak
to sunset they journey

erect on their raft till they reach their end.
All day they carry our remains
and wear our faces.

                    *

Today the branches
they carry are huge,
double a man's length.

You can see it in their eyes.

Other days they carry
nothing.  Still their
shoulders weigh heavy.

                    *

The mudflats at dawn
moulded like lava
carry the imprints of feeding birds

but sucking the rising tide
are larger holes. Who
has passed before me?

*

Sometimes behind the men
often leading them
(you will see her shadow)

 – the memory-bearer.

Out of an assembly of bones
her breasts sway
like dry leaves.

Listen to the wind blow through them.

At low tide you can follow
her footprints only so far.

vi)

That man's borders are menaced.
He can feel it in the wire and sticks
that are his bones.

He will defend what's his
with all he's got,
with every thistle, every clod.

The horizon, split by mist,
streams towards him
and he's posed to meet

the marauders head-on
but he himself is beyond the pale.
He's of the marshlands.

With that mashed-up face
you can tell
he's not one of us.

vii)

The bandages binding his calves
flap round his ankles. He strides on,
white with dust, has places to go,
far from the marshlands.

He hitches a ride, sits up
beside the driver and from there
he sees the motorway split
in two, its lanes vanishing
out of time.

The man won't look back.
Heading for the city, he has work to do.
He'll be dropped off in a place
he may have known once

and dreamed of returning to,
now a dry land of crowded crossroads
where silence is gone and neon lights
are too strong for his deep-scored eyes.

In the dim corner of a railway station
you'll come across him, a heap,
his crooked branch-arm stretched out.

viii)

Holding tight to his own
morality, sensing that
the gluttony of corpses
in forests beyond the barrows
must stop, he seeks
a new order to follow.

Peering into the intricacies
of roots, their creases
and folds, their under-earth
architecture, he ponders
their complexities but mud
silts his understanding.

One day he'll crumble
and collapse without warning
into an unseemly heap
while from the kiln will step
his twin, fired into bronze,
sleek and shining.

ix)

And if these gods walk out on us one day
with their league-long strides, leaving

this land of herons and silky oyster-catchers,
of wetness and wings, to join a wider world

 – if they come across our wayfarers on the road,
will they carry the orphans on their backs?

Look at their faces, battered and smeared
and, for that, human. Let them walk on.

# III Interiors

**interiors**

the birds are filled with trees

listen to the drip
              of sap
and swish of branches
                         in their soft throats

*

        sky enters earth
via a lake's portal

        fish replete with rivers
                   ripple together

*

after a great
         disgorging

hills and valleys
                   swap places

*

cradled inside a child's cry
           a mother's rage

*

our homes are stacked inside us
       brick on brick

family and friends
       move about the rooms.

**Ode to a Brain**

Comic, tuberous, your knobbly surface
like a crumpled tissue, your humps
and lumps, your creases,
your gyri, folds and fissures,
your hemispheres of lobes: frontal,
parietal, temporal, occipital.

Once a nerve centre splendid on its stem,
a universe of neural networks
tree-like in heavenly forests
with your floaty connections
now shrunk to the size of a fist
frozen and pickled in your labelled jar.
Cerebellum, corpus callosum.

Whose memories skidded or fumbled
down your perforant paths? Whose pain
did you gird around? Whom did you teach,
deep in Broca's Area, from that bean,
that worm, that curled thing,
words to write and sing?

**The box**

Here's a wooden box with a glass door – through it you can see rooms as in a dolls' house. There's a switch attached to a battery to turn the light on or off. A narrow staircase links two floors. Downstairs are Mother and Father (so small, so far away). He's on the sofa and she's walking out of the room. They may have had an argument. Upstairs are Mother's parents in their own living room. Mother's Father is silent, dividing his roll-up with a razor blade. His wife is composing a lullaby, humming it to herself in German. Behind him, even with the light on, is darkness. There, all the other figures are invisible, except to him.

## Topography of Terror, Berlin.

The banners hang ten foot high between
the linden trees leading to the *schloss*:
photographs of the old, each eyelid seen
close-up with double fold. Features of loss:

they are my grandfather's face, each one.
Through these memorials Berlin remembers and I
remember him, silent, refuged in London
in his great chair, can feel the hang of his dry

tired cheeks, smell the tobacco from his sliced
cigarettes. In the hubbub of his city,
above the noise of tourists, I strain to hear

his voice among fragments, search the archives
of terror near the broken wall, find the pity
in records of eliminations and in the fear.

\*

Nor can I ignore those arms held high
and straight among massed exultant crowds
as women with shaven heads are paraded by
on wooden carts, or be deaf to their loud

hateful voices (once more become familiar?)
On this journey not all I'm searching for
is what I want to find. I travelled here
on a path meant to lead to never more.

A German standing by a *Neues Volk* poster,
turning to me in tears, says *Das ist schrecklich*!
I try to say we must learn from it, instead

I say I'm sorry, not knowing if for him
or myself or the ones in the poster,
the others, who are already condemned.

## Carl

dark matter won't interact
with other matter

each of us has our own
matter — my darkness

is invisible and in a dull world
it doesn't glow

on occasions it streams out
through the eyes

          \*

he sought shadow
when the light was too harsh

shadow is not as precise
as the thing casting it

the edges are blurred
his edges were blurred

he carried too much weight
we lost sight of him

          \*

sometimes he'd take a train
far from the city

shelter in the shade of an oak tree
later he left home

to sleep in doorways
shadow is blocked light

## Sliding pebbles

He strips off his vest
and with his sandaled feet
tests the beach pebbles
– as if they might
without warning

slide away from him –
then stands hands on hips
staring out to sea
determining whether
to go in and how.

His leg muscles are wasted,
feet and ankles swollen
though the wide span of his back
will once have held power.
He reminds me of my father.

## Lorenzo Lotto's Portraits

*Sometimes in museums the paints speak to me*
*And irony suddenly vanishes*
'Self-portrait' by Adam Zagajevski

i)

On the *condottiere's* fingers
are two rings – one was
recently worn by his wife.

His right hand covers a small
skull scattered with petals:
rose and jasmine,

love and purity.
His other hand rests over
his spleen: site of melancholy.

ii)

Is it the ledger lying open
on a green cloth that prompts
this youth's anxiety, his skin

moon-like against the dark sky
of his hair?  Rose petals are
on his table too and letters,

a ring and a shawl, gold-fringed,
with a lizard half-hidden in its folds,
symbol of resurrection.

Has he rejected his old world
of the lute and hunting horn still
hanging on the shadowed wall?

iii)

Each portrait reflects the desolation
of the painter's gaze, whether
in the face of friar or goldsmith
or witness to the crucifixion.
Downward and inward his regard.

Light plays on the canvas:
flesh-tones impastoed
in the grooves, capillaries
around the nose. Lean in close
as if to your bathroom mirror.

**The back of transparency**

*after Mira Schendel*

little nothings

a constellation of signs

letters

frail as air

to be read from both sides

on rice paper

hanging between us

yet we lean forward together

to see the

opacity and transparency

black on white

word and silence

always back to the word

and silence

*

in a Chinese landscape dominated by high mountains gorges giant trees
and waterfalls the eye is drawn always to the little man with his backpack
occasionally leading his donkey

a scroll can be read horizontally backwards or forwards or vertically with
the script running down

you have to search for the man     he doesn't appear at once

you're allowed time to wonder at the grandness of creation
its deadly energy    then you gasp with relief          There

you lean forward again          There he is


*


Her lines of linked

**AAA**s flee across the nocturnal landscape of Itatiaia

words down to the minimum

*vida   sim*

## Goethe in Rome

He looks out of the window
of the second floor room of
number 18 (of course I can't see
what absorbs him in Via del Corso).
One shutter is closed; sunlight
slices across his hunched
shoulders, contrasting with
the dark wash you've used
for the rest of his back
and the room walls.

You've painted the floor pattern
precisely; its geometry emphasises
the curve of his slim figure
as he shifts weight onto his left leg
and leans his elbows on the window ledge.
His white trousers, buttoned at the knee,
fall loosely, shirt partly out,
hair barely tied.  He's losing
the slipper on his right foot
as he's about to move forward —

Now I see what he sees:
hawkers everywhere, the old woman
who stands on the street corner
until she's sold her few onions
and garlic folded in cloth;
half-naked children chasing
each other perilously close
to the hooves of horses
pulling their carriages over basalt
cobbles so fast that sparks flash.

He leans further out to catch hold
of the light bouncing back to him
from amber house walls, red roof
alive against the sky and he'll store
the colours, add them to the chart
propped up by his journal of poems.

## Notes

Most of the places in Italy referred to in this collection are in the central region of Le Marche.

**I Faultlines**: the poems in pp 22 – 39 of this section were written in response to the earthquakes that shook central Italy in August and again in October 2016. Over 300 died, many more were injured and lost their homes.

**Patriotism**: Fascist shooting of six African migrants in Macerata on 3 February 2018.

**Emanuel:** this racial attack occurred in the town of Fermo on July 7 2016.

**All out to sea:** written on June 24$^{th}$ 2016, the day after the European referendum in the UK.

**Visso:** a small town in the Sibillini mountains was badly damaged but, unlike in other towns closer to the epicentre, no lives were lost.

**Water now** and **Regina Aquarium** refer to the drought in Rome, summer 2017

**Moka**: September 2017: the 'supervolcano' at Campi Flegrei, Naples, was reported to be showing dangerous signs of eruption.

**II The Creek Men**: the sequence in this section was inspired by Laurence Edwards' sculptures to be found in the landscape of East Anglia. They include a group of three bronzes called The Creek Men and A Thousand Tides, a prone figure in a lagoon among reed-beds that can only be seen when the tide is out, and other individual works.

Information about the 'Creek Men' sculptures can be found here: (*http://laurenceedwardssculpture.com.*)

**Topography of Terror**: exhibition and documentation centre built on the site of former Gestapo and SS headquarters in Berlin. *Neues Volk* was a mass-market illustrated Nazi magazine. *Das ist shrechlich* – 'That's horrible' in German.

**Ode to a brain**: prompted by the Wellcome Collection's 2012/13 exhibition, *Death: a self-portrait.*

**The back of transparency**: born in 1919 in Switzerland, the artist Mira Schendel moved to Italy where, under Mussolini, she was stripped of her citizenship due to her Jewish heritage and she eventually lived as an exile in Brazil. *Vida Sim* means *Life Yes* in Portuguese.

**Goethe in Rome:** written in response to *Goethe am Fenster seiner Wohnung in Rom,* a sketch by Johann Heinrich Wilhelm Tischbein (1751-1829)

# About the Author

Photo: Dahlaina Jones

Caroline Maldonado has written both fiction and poetry and received a Writing MA at Sheffield Hallam University in 2008. Her poems have appeared in many journals, online and in anthologies and she has won or been placed in several competitions.

For seven years until 2016 she chaired the Board of Trustees of *Modern Poetry in Translation.* She has curated a selection of Italian poetry online for *The High Window* (https://thehighwindowpress.com/2021/09/18/italian-3/ )

Her pamphlet *What they say in Avenale* was published by Indigo Dreams Publishing (2014). Her translations from Italian published by Smokestack Books include *Your call keeps us awake*, poems by Rocco Scotellaro, co-translated with Allen Prowle (2013); *Isabella* (Smokestack Books 2019) which includes Maldonado's own poems with translations of poems by the Renaissance poet, Isabella Morra; and poems by Laura Fusco: *'Liminal* (2020), winner of the 2019 UK PEN Translation award, and *Nadir* (2022).

In August 2019 the Poetry Book Society recommended *Isabella* in their 'Women in Translation' initiative as one of the five best poetry books translated by women in 2018/19. It was also commended in the University of Warwick's international prize for 'Women in Translation' and selected as one of *The Morning Star*'s Best Poetry collections 2019.

**Some reviews of Caroline Maldonado's writing:**

**On *What they say in Avenale*:**

An extraordinary and exhilarating way of seeing

Allen Prowle, *Saboteur*

Beautiful, evocative poems with a lightness to them and a careful precision – nothing seems excess, all the words feel weighed placed…a consummate performance, altogether.

Sasha Dugdale

**On *Isabella*:**

Taken together, Maldonado's introduction, her translations of Morra and her own poems of discovery constitute a superbly integrated whole which provides powerful testimony to the transcendence of art in even the most dourly unfavourable circumstances.

David Cooke, *The North.*

I applaud Maldonado for her gracious sharing, shrewd observation and linguistic skills. This poet has attentively taken Morra's work, loyally giving the voiceless a vociferous writing life whilst, in solidarity, wrapping her own voice around it.

Julie Hogg, *London Grip* 'Isabella'

As she has surely done in producing this fascinating little book, Maldonado intends to give Morra a voice in many of these new poems and, in 'Scirocco', we hear this imprisoned young woman poignantly repeating, "*Who will ever hear me?*" Both translator and publisher are to be congratulated in this recovering of an almost lost female voice from Renaissance Italy.

Martyn Crucefix